I Made It Out

Volume Two

John P. Kee
Charlotte, North Carolina

Volume Two

Copyright ©2021 John P. Kee

All rights reserved. No part of this selection may be reproduced or transmitted in any form or by any means, electrical or mechanical, without written permission from the publisher.

Publisher: John P. Kee
Front Cover Design: Zvikomborero Zed Rwodzi, Keyanna Schoenholz, and John P. Kee
Contributor: Rekeita Bradford
Editor: Shana C. Williams of ULEP, LLC (www.ulep247.com)

First Edition
Printed in the United States of America

DEDICATION

For many, 2020 was a very challenging year. From experiencing Covid-19, unemployment, and the loss of loved ones. No one suspected how this Global Pandemic would affect us all. It will be a part of history, taught for generations to come.

Though we are in a New Year, some are still finding it difficult to adjust to this new norm. As I sit here, I think about what's going on in the world. I began to read the chapters of "I Made It Out, Volume II." I was encouraged by the depth of revelation and oil poured out from these contributing authors. They wrote as if they knew the time and the season we were entering; all the chapters were written before the pandemic. I stand amazed at the perfect timing of God!

I dedicate this book to all those affected by the pandemic. To all, finding it hard to navigate through life issues. I speak a new season in your life. Prepare yourselves for a time of healing, realigning, and most of all a refreshing.

For the Bible declares in 1 John 5:4, *"For whatsoever is born of God overcometh the world: and this is the victory that overcometh the world, event our faith."*

I leave you with this, faith will not only bring you out. But it will be the foundation on which we stand!

"We made it out!"

Your brother in the faith,
-Pastor John P. Kee

Volume Two

FOREWORD

According to Plato, "Music gives soul to the universe, wings to the mind, flight to the imagination, and life to everything." If Plato is correct then music gives soul, wings, flight, and life. Music adds to who we are. It releases us into far lands, untouched by mundane existential dilemmas. It invites us into new dimensions of beauty and serenity.

For decades, Pastor John P. Kee ministered the lyrics of gospel music from the wells of his pains and the fountains of his joys. As we listen, we are reminded, "Life and Favor" is upon us. As we close our eyes in the sanctuaries of our souls, we know that "Jesus is Real." God will always "Rain on Us." Each chapter of this book is a song title. Pastor Kee graciously extends an invitation. Dive into the spiritual and Biblical implications of the gospel songs God has given to him.

Gospel music, in its essence, is music that brings "good news". Corruption and bigotry are ever present in this world's politics. We need some "good news". During this pandemic, society needs a reprieve. Due to injustice, families are wondering if their children will return home safely. As you hold this book, know that you have some "good news" in your hands. Allow the chapters to lift you from any broken shambles. Look unto the Lord for stability.

Volume Two

Allow this volume to lift you from your reality to glimpse into eternity. Reality is limited, spatial, and finite. Eternity is unlimited, boundless, and infinite. Allow the testimonies shared minister to you. I pray that your testimony will be, "I Made It Out!"

-Bishop Reginald W. Sharpe, Jr.

TABLE OF CONTENTS

CHAPTER 1: TO BE LOVED — 1
-Elder Shelby Talton — *13*

CHAPTER 2: MIGHTY, YES YOU ARE — 15
-Pastor Kimberly Ray-Gavin — *19*

CHAPTER 3: ONE GOD — 21
-Pastor Jathan Austin — *28*

CHAPTER 4: RESPECT — 29
- Bishop Herbert C. Crump, Jr. — *33*

CHAPTER 5: STILL IN THE FIGHT — 35
-Elder Jeff Davis — *43*

CHAPTER 6: HE WILL NEVER FORSAKE ME — 45
-Dr. Terrell Fletcher — *50*

CHAPTER 7: YOUR HIGHER WAYS — 51
-Elder Leven Wilson — *60*

CHAPTER 8: MOVING ON — 61
-Pastor Derrick L. McRae — *67*

CHAPTER 9: LORD, I'M WILLING — 69
- Pastor Darrell Blair — *78*

CHAPTER 10: I'M YET CONFIDENT — 79
-Minister Daniel Sutton — *85*

CHAPTER 11: HE PREPARED ME — 87
-Dr. Derrick J. Hughes — *94*

CHAPTER 12: LIVE AGAIN — 95
-Bishop Ezekiel Newton — *102*

CHAPTER 13: KNOW YOUR STORY — 103
-Pastor Kelvin De'Marcus Allen — *111*

Volume Two

CHAPTER 14: ONE YES AWAY **113**
    -BISHOP RANDY BORDERS *120*

CHAPTER 15: TRUST HIM **121**
    -MINISTER EBONY MARIE PETTY *126*

CHAPTER 16: TAKE THE RISK **127**
    -BISHOP GREG DAVIS *135*

CHAPTER 17: I FORGIVE YOU **137**
    - MINISTER L. SPENSER SMITH *147*

I Made It Out

CHAPTER 1: TO BE LOVED

Volume Two

The word 'to' is a preposition used for expressing motion or direction toward a point, person, place, or thing approached and reached. 'Be' simply implies existence. The title suggests being in a position of going after, seeking, or heading in the direction of an existence in a place where there is complete attachment, euphoric intensity, and deep affection.

Biblically that place would be filled with patience, kindness, forgiveness, well wishes, generosity, and restoration despite failures and faults. 1 Corinthians 13:4-5, *"Love is patient, love is kind. It does not envy, it does not boast, it is not proud. It does not dishonor others, it is not self-seeking, it is not easily angered, it keeps no record of wrongs."* We desire to exist in the atmosphere of kindness, encouragement, and honor.

When referencing being loved, we need to clearly define our approach. Are we discussing love for God or love by God? The Greek term "theophilia" means the love or favor of God. Theophilos means, "Friend of God," originally in the sense of being loved by God. In this chapter, it is necessary to discuss being loved by God.

Volume Two

As I understand it, there is no way to properly show love for God or anyone else until we have a better understanding of what it means to be loved by God. Love from this position rather is not like falling in or seeking out love, as it applies to our fleshly understanding and desires. What will cause us to experience, cherish, accept, express, and give love, regardless of who we are, or language spoken. God is love and we were made to be loved by Him.

> Genesis 1:26-27 KJV, reads, *"And God said, Let us make man in our image, after our likeness: and let them have dominion over the fish of the sea, and over the fowl of the air, and over the cattle, and over all the earth, and over every creeping thing that creepeth upon the earth."*

This Word clearly tells us that we are created in the image of God. We were placed above all other earthly creatures. This distinction grants us incredible capabilities. Many live their lives clueless as to whom they are in God. You are gifted. 2 Peter 1:3 KJV, *"According to his divine power hath given unto us all things that pertain unto life and godliness, through the knowledge of him that hath called us to glory and virtue."* He loved us so much from the beginning that He gave us divine connection and power and set us apart for Himself. 1 John 4:8 KJV, *"He that loveth not knoweth not God; for God is love."*

<u>Fun Fact:</u>
The word is the present tense third-person singular of be, these words are equal in meaning.

Our ability to love should be Christ-like. Our struggle is learning how to love but in accepting the way we have been loved with the same love has been poured into us. We fight 'to do' and 'to be' what we define as love. True acceptance is understanding who we are created to be and who we are to God. First and foremost, accept that we are and were created to be loved by Him.

Our love walk will improve immediately when we function from the existence of being loved by Him. We must accept that we were made, and we are loved by Him. This is the catalyst that unlocks our willingness to exist in the space described in 1 Corinthians. Our capacity to love properly in our human condition is incomplete. It can be hindered by our lack of understanding concerning our divine nature. Our divine nature supersedes our human nature. To be loved by God fills us with the ability to love, like Him.

Though we have a capacity to love, many of us do not understand what love really is. We do not know how to love. We certainly will never be able to love properly without submitting to God's Spirit living within us. Even then, it is a process that takes some a lifetime. I recommend two books written by Andrew Murray, "The Blessings of Obedience" and "The Master's Indwelling."

It requires starting over and being willing to unlearn many learned behaviors, worldly expectations, and concepts of love. We must be taught or educated all over again about what love really is. We must learn how to receive God's love and give it. These instructions come directly from God's Word: *"Sanctify them through thy truth: thy word is truth"* (John 17:17 KJV).

> There are many truths that show us the mind of Christ as it pertains to love, *"He that hath my commandments, and keepeth them, he it is that loveth me: and he that loveth me shall be loved of my Father, and I will love him, and will manifest myself to him."* (John 14:21 KJV).

Loving God requires obedience. This is where our 'to do' part comes into play. We must surrender to obedience. Willingness to obey changes our thinking and our understanding and allows us to experience, accept and imitate true Godly love in our lives. Our capacity to obey is the magnet that brings Biblical reality into our existence.

There is no way to discuss love without discussing obedience. There is no way to fully access His promises without having a heart that validates the words of Jesus in Luke 22:42, *"Saying, Father, if thou be willing, remove this cup from me: nevertheless not my will, but thine, be done."*

God placed within us a need to give and receive love. *"For God so loved the world, that he gave his only begotten Son, that whosoever believeth in him should not perish, but have everlasting life."* (John 3:16 KJV). We focus on receiving and getting when it comes to love. We have already been given unto. Many pray God, send it to me or get it for me. A constant state of mind seems to be, I need, I want, if only I had love, and so on. Your task is to be loved by the one who created you and function from a position of give rather than receive. Then you will become the magnet that creates the reality and atmosphere that you have always had access to and were created to exist in.

> *"Give, and it shall be given unto you; good measure, pressed down, and shaken together, and running over, shall men give into your bosom. For with the same measure that ye mete withal it shall be measured to you again."* (Luke 6:38 KJV).

Volume Two

To love like Christ, I should get no credit for the ability. That is who God is to me. He is going to love me right, *"For whom the Lord loveth he chasteneth, and scourgeth every son whom he receiveth."* (Hebrews 12:6 KJV). This means, the Lord is going to give me a hug. He is going to get me straight but then He will provide for me. All I need and He will fill me with so much of His love that I cannot help myself.

I must love because I am blessed and full of love. I am benefitted by it and I am grateful. I am indebted and I know He should get all the credit. *"What is man, that thou art mindful of him? And the son of man, that thou visitest him?"* (Psalms 8:4 KJV). You will recognize that you are full of love. Your own need and desire to show love, will not be able to be denied because it will be running over.

To be loved causes you to give love. Satan got involved in man's reasoning and added a dose of jealousy and selfishness. Satan perverted God's way of love, he distorted God's way of giving. Satan's job is to twist everything in the opposite direction of God's will, and he stays on his assignment. God gave and He gives.

"According as his divine power hath given unto us all things that pertain unto life and godliness, through the knowledge of him that hath called us to glory and virtue." (2 Peter 1:3 KJV).

Jackie Wilson performed, "To Be Loved" a song written by Roquel "Billy" Davis, Gwen Gordy Fuqua, and Berry Gordy. The song defined the love for which a man was searching. I can testify that God is and has been more than all these things to me. To be loved by Him is better than the best thing I ever experienced and the best day I can try to describe.

There are selfless people in this world, some more than others. There are also selfish people in this world. I attend New Life Fellowship where people serve the helpless and hopeless. I was blessed to start SWAAT which serves the same dynamic. Many people serve in both entities. Many volunteer to assist the poor and needy, those hospitalized, hurting, wounded and in prison, as we should.

Very often these acts of kindness are done with an expectation of getting something in return. Those that have no desire to get in return are operating from the position of 'running over'. Some are functioning from the place where they have completely surrendered to be loved by God. They have no lack, so they need no further reward.

> *"Then shall the King say unto them on his right hand, Come, ye blessed of my Father, inherit the kingdom prepared for you from the foundation of the world: For I was an hungered, and ye gave me meat: I was thirsty, and ye gave me drink: I was a stranger, and ye took me in: Naked, and ye clothed me: I was sick, and ye visited me: I was in prison, and ye came unto me. Then shall the righteous answer him, saying, Lord, when saw we thee an hungered, and fed thee? Or thirsty, and gave thee drink? When saw we thee a stranger, and took thee in? Or naked, and clothed thee? Or when saw we thee sick, or in prison, and came unto thee? And the King shall answer and say unto them, Verily I say unto you, Inasmuch as ye have done it unto one of the least of these my brethren, ye have done it unto me."* (Matthew 25:34-40 KJV).

God's love is in us. It is given when we surrender to be loved by Him and receive Him, His Holy Spirit. We were made to be God-like in how we love. We cannot do it properly without His Spirit to lead and direct us in our purpose. As Disciples of Christ we should concern ourselves not to miss the mark of God. Our purpose, we were made to become love as He is. We were made to give love as He does. We were made to be loved and to love. I get it! Finally, I get it! Here comes my praise break, "To be loved. To be loved. Oh, what a feeling."

I Made It Out

I am no longer trying to 'to be love.' With this understanding, I have reached the place of acceptance that allows me to be loved. There is no effort needed or action to be taken. There is no requirement to do on my part. I just accept whom made me and who He made me like! My humble prayer is to continue in His wisdom and guidance concerning the matter and that I have shared something that points you like an arrow to this existence in Him. I hear it! Do you? Sighs of relief, beautiful music. I feel it, do you? Ultimate elation, breaths used to energize gut busting laughter, chest filling joy, face stretching smiles. I am consumed by it!

My husband recently asked me about breath taking moments in my life. This is one! The moment this realization struck me. I have the thing that is most important to me. I am, what I have been running after, reaching for, approaching, and heading in the direction of my whole life. Those who know me or have encountered me for a few days, have heard the phrase, "Be love" but God's revelation in 2019 has coined a new phrase for me. The distinct ability to genuinely 'be love' will only come from the wisdom or understanding of what it means to be loved.

Volume Two

Each of us wants to be loved. We should. We were created as the object of His love and to be loved by Him. The revelation here is that you are. My new phrase is, "Be Loved!" We house and can be filled with what we somehow become convinced we must pursue. All the love of God offers us is true. It is a game changer, freedom, success, stability, and strength. It is God's gift and reward. It is the ability to obey Him. It is bliss! It is the ability to receive His love and the ability to give His love.

Do you want your love walk to glorify God? Do you want every relationship in your life to improve? How will you act when you realize there is no need to wrestle, doubt, struggle, or maneuver, with God? Who He says, He is. Are you willing to believe He can give you just what He said He would give you? I challenge you to be guided to a place of resolve that accepts His all-consuming care, comfort, guidance, and provision. I encourage you to accept the kind of love that has been waiting to be received by you without battle since you took your very first breath of life.

Present and submit yourself to be loved by God. If you question how, understand Peter was the only disciple that ever walked on water. Why, the answer is simple, he was the only one who asked. *"And Peter answered him and said, Lord, if it be thou, bid me come unto thee on the water."* (Matthew 14:28 KJV). If you are struggling ask, "Lord, teach me how to be loved." *"Ask, and it shall be given you; seek, and ye shall find; knock, and it shall be opened unto you"* (Matthew 7:7 KJV). It is the best decision you will ever make.

-*Elder Shelby Talton*

Volume Two

CHAPTER 2: MIGHTY, YES YOU ARE

Volume Two

I Made It Out

One of the things I absolutely love about God is that He is Almighty! He is the creator of heaven and earth. He has all might and power. He is the eternal God. With His voice, He spoke the universe into existence. When we speak of His might, we are reminded that God Almighty is El Shaddai: "God, the all-powerful one." He performs wonders. His infinite wisdom testifies of His unlimited power.

I would like to continue speaking of His might. It is so powerful. In the times when tempestuous storms rise, He has authority over the winds and the waves. They must obey His will. He is the King of Heaven, the builder of everything. He is a wonder, and His name are Holy. Mighty, yes you are, Lord!

Throughout the historic, prophetic, and poetical pages of the Bible, we discover the truth. Our mighty God is omnipotent, omniscient, and omnipresent. Mighty, yes you are! He has ultimate power. He can do exceeding and abundantly above all that we can ask or think.

It is fascinating to consider. Despite our mighty God's monumental vastness, He has the uncanny ability to hear our cry and to respond to our slightest whisper. God loves us and He is on our side. Father, mighty, yes you are!

The Lord has given us a beautiful gift called the power of intercession. It is an honor to have a passionate conversation with God. Intercessory prayer is the great privilege of seeking an audience with Almighty God. It is to render a petition, supplication, or a prayer request on behalf of others who desperately need His intervention. God is a bridge over troubled waters and will hear and answer our faintest plea.

What a comfort it is to know that when we call Him, He will answer. Thank you, God, for proving yourself; for walking with us and for being on our side. He is a strong deliverer. He breaks yolks, fetters, and chains. He does miracles. He raises the bowed down head. He heals the sick and sets the captives free. He gives joy unspeakable and full of glory. Mighty, yes you are!

I praise the Lord for being the everlasting God. I testify that there is no one before Him and no one like Him. He stepped out of nowhere onto nothing and created humanity. I lift my hands, leap for joy and I rejoice. I praise Him with my whole heart. Thank you for my victory, freedom, and my deliverance.

Psalm 46: 1-3, *"God is our refuge and strength..."* the source of our lives and strength. He is the joy that abides deep within. He is a well that never runs dry. The fruit of my lips give Him praise. Mighty, yes you are. *"Keep me as the apple of the eye, hide me under the shadow of thy wings"* (Psalm 17:8). I will declare to the world, "Oh God you are mighty! Oh, yes you are!"

-Pastor Kimberly Ray-Gavin

Volume Two

CHAPTER 3: ONE GOD

Volume Two

I admonish you, "Have faith in God". In 2005, Time Magazine did a cover story entitled "The God Gene." It was an expose on research being studied in over a dozen universities in the United States. Different researchers in different universities from California to New York are all looking into the same question: Does our DNA compel us to seek a higher power?

The remarkable part of this study is the researchers say, "Yes." Does that surprise you? To be honest I was a bit surprised. Not so much by what the researchers found, but that they agreed that to some point we are all looking for a higher power; someone else to be in control. We have a deep longing for there to be someone, something to guide our paths and to give us hope. That longing does not just reside in the world. We struggle with it in the church as well.

Blasé Pascal was a French philosopher, known for his work in Math and Chemistry. At age 12, he discovered the Principles of Geometry. At 16, he wrote "The Geometry of Conics." He also invented a calculating machine and the theory of probability. In his mid-thirties, Pascal became interested in religion. He penned the theory scientists are trying to prove today. He wrote, "Within each one of us there is a God-shaped vacuum that only God can fill." If that is true, then every one of us was made to seek out God.

Growing up in the church I was taught indirectly what it meant to seek out God. I watched elders, deacons, and Bible school teachers profess with their lives, "If you want to fill the God-shaped vacuum in your life then what you needed to do is find God's will for your life and follow it perfectly." The difference with this generation versus the generation before me, is they were taught to have faith in God. Somehow, our current generation has moved away from having faith in God to just having faith.

Religion has become like the Nike™ quote 'Just Do it.' The church today says, "Just Have Faith." Many are losing their faith in God because God is no longer the center of our faith. Unfortunately, my generation is self-centered and almost narcissistic. Their focus is on individual success and worldly passions. Ambition is the new relationship with God.

Spiritual narcissism controls the messages of faith today. Culture seeks to alter the message of faith and construct a different kind of God. One that is tolerant of all human behaviors. Philippians 2:10-11 says, *"That at the name of Jesus every knee should bow, of those heaven, and of those on earth, and of those under the earth, and that every tongue should confess that Jesus Christ is Lord, to the glory of God the Father."*

No matter how hard this generation tries to ignore, refute, or deny there is only one God. It will never change the fact that our savior Christ Jesus remains God of all things. This generation must be delivered from crisis faith. Often, people only respond or engage God when they are in trouble. Their circumstances have overwhelmed them.

I pray we can retrain our generation to have the kind faith that always engages our Lord and call Him the true and living God. I pray our relationship with Christ will go deeper than our trouble and reach into the depths of souls to that gives all lives real meaning. The nature of this generation is rooted in convenience and not commitment.

Volume Two

Commitment must go beyond, feelings, schedules, and a 'to-do' list. Over the last 25 years, we got away from preaching about whom God is and having faith in His son Jesus. Consequently, people started building their faith around themselves or their limited abilities. When circumstances rocked their lives, it rocked their faith.

This generation teaches to have faith in yourself and faith in your success. There is some truth in this belief. However, if your faith in yourself is not rooted in a proper understanding of Christ, your faith is worthless! To prevent our faith from becoming tossed by the winds of the sea, our anchor must be in Jesus. The scriptures are clear we must have faith in God. Instead of teaching faith in God, we ended up doing many a disservice by only teach to have faith.

Who is God? Elohim means "God." This name refers to God's incredible power and might. He is the One and only God. He is Supreme, the true God in a world that promotes many false gods and religions. He is the one on whom we can fully rely. He is Sovereign. He is the one we can completely trust. He is the Mighty One over all of nature, this world, and the heavens above, our creative God who has worked wonders by His hands.

Yahweh means "The Lord." Yahweh is derived from the Hebrews word for "I Am." It is the proper name of the divine person. It is from the verb which means to exist or be. When God told Moses to go to Pharaoh and to lead the Israelites out of Egypt, Moses was scared. He needed reassurance, He needed to know God was bigger than this problem, that He would carry them through. Even if people would not listen to Him, they would listen to the One who sent Him. God's name carried that much awe and honor.

> Moses said to God, "*Suppose I go to the Israelites and say to them, The God of you fathers has sent me to you, and they ask me, "What is His name?" Then what shall tell them?"* God said to Moses, "*I AM, WHO I AM. This is what you are to say to the Israelites, "I AM has sent me to you."* (Exodus 3:13-14)

Abba means "Daddy, Father." Abba is the most intimate form of God's name. It shows us His character as our loving daddy. He is the One who can be fully trusted. Christ is clearly in scripture the only one God that becomes all we need. He is in all, over us all, and through us all. Other cultures and religions seek many gods. Christ Jesus is all enough lacking nothing and withholding nothing from His children. He is our guide, protector, shelter, refuge, healer, salvation, and God. He is the only true God!

Out of all the names to understand who Christ is, Abba is the most important. It speaks to His true nature as our Father. He is unrivaled in being the author of all things. He is zealous about the care and keep of His children. He is jealous at the thought of being replaced in the hearts of His children. He is unwavering in assuring the safety of all who serves Him. He is the one and only true God!

-Pastor Jathan Austin

CHAPTER 4: RESPECT

Volume Two

We are at a critical moment in the history of humanity. I believe the heart of humanity has hardened. As a result, there is a diminished display of personal and professional respect. It is noticeable throughout many facets of our society. Some expect politicians to push the boundaries of respect as they vie for political position. However, no one expected our political leaders to eagerly abandon decency and morality in the name of political power and policy.

This same sentiment is in businesses. Banking institutions fabricate financial portfolios to impress investors. Simultaneously, they place customers under an avalanche of insurmountable debt. I have grown to accept; people are not motivated by the same spiritual source. Their behavior reflects their beliefs. The lack of respect shown may be their way of saying, "You haven't earned my respect."

My concern for our society is not isolated to the actions of our, political leaders or the financial industry. Unfortunately, it includes our faith community. Within the ranks of the religious is where I find it most difficult to bear. I humbly believe there is a growing lack of respect towards the divine deity of our great God.

Volume Two

Growing up I was always taught to respect the word of God and the things of God. This teaching was instilled in me. An unwavering commitment to always acknowledge God as divine royalty and the church as His place of abode. I was taught not to use the name of God in vain nor to speak of God in a demeaning manner. The physical church, a man-made structure was God's dwelling place and to be respected.

Over the past few decades, I noticed a decline in how we respect all that represents God. People who were drinking or smoking on a street corner would see a church mother, deacon, or preacher walking pass. They would place their beverages and cigarettes behind their backs as a sign of respect. There was a joy in the hearts of parishioners when cleaning the church or helping set up for an upcoming worship experience.

During those days, we respected God based on how we viewed God. We believed and gladly received God as a friend. We revered God as a Father. I wholeheartedly believe, God the Father has earned our perpetual display of respect. He sacrificed His son Jesus to experience a brutal death to offer salvation to a sin filled society. Therefore, we should not degrade God to be our 'homeboy'. We must work to keep His name holy.

In the words of the neo-classical poet Bryan C. Williams, more affectionately known as Birdman, "I believe it's time for the each of us to… Put some respect on [H]is name!"

- Bishop Herbert C. Crump, Jr.

Volume Two

CHAPTER 5: STILL IN THE FIGHT

Volume Two

I often reflect on I Timothy 6:12. The scripture instructs us to *"Fight the good fight of faith..."* To a believer, that really says a lot! It is a plan, a promise. It has purpose. It is challenging and encouraging. What I like most about this verse is, it is a command. To all of those who have decided to follow Jesus, fight! It is His guarantee. Yes, we are in a fight. But your strength comes from His mighty power from within. Therefore, you will not lose! It is written in Ephesians, *"We must put on all the armor of God..."* It empowers us to stand safe against all the strategies and tricks of Satan.

Remember, we are not fighting against flesh and blood. We are fighting against bodiless evil rulers of an unseen world, satanic beings, mighty powers of darkness, and wicked evil spirits in the heavenly places. It is a fixed fight, so gather up what you will need to win! Ephesians 6:14-17 speaks of armor to resist the enemy in the time of evil. It mentions a strong belt, breastplate, good shoes, shield, helmet, and the sword are needed for the fight. Verse 18 seals it with prayer which is essential in this ongoing warfare.

Volume Two

Pray a little longer and you will last a lot longer! Spend more time with Him and you will become empowered in Him. I advise you to read Ephesians 6:11-18. Enjoy the empowerment it brings to your life. The mind is the battlefield. Let us look at what might hold us hostage. What makes us slow to act on His promises? If we are honest, it might be difficult at times to determine who or what it is we really believe. Much less, can we explain it to someone else?

We have all been there. Let us just call it the planning, preparation, and training stages for battle. Some might ask what is faith? Why in the world should I fight for it? What is a born-again believer? These questions may also unveil the enemy at hand because faith in the Savior destroys denial and doubt. It exposes betrayal. *"Faith assures us of what we hope for and convinces us of things we have never seen"* (Hebrews 11:1).

Make a list of things you believe but have not seen yet, simply put, that's faith. We have not seen God through direct visual contact. We did not witness creation. We did not observe the sin of Adam and Eve. We did not witness the birth of Christ. We did not see Him die on the cross nor witness His resurrection. These are all things we believe but have not seen. When we believe and affirm as truth all we have not seen, that is faith.

We are fighting for what we are sure of, which is our faith. Our belief and our hope, which ultimately is eternal life with Him. This is the life of the believer trusting in the promises of God. His faithfulness and love. A born-again believer is an individual redeemed by the precious blood of Jesus through repentance. They are cleansed of all their sins. They become an immediate candidate for the Holy Spirit. They continue to walk and live in total obedience to His word.

This will make them different. To fight the good fight of faith also means to work hard, strive, and hold fast to your faith without wavering. We must be centered and anchored in His word, not our own. Romans 12:2 addresses conformity. Check out the entire chapter. The fight is forever changing. It is evolving, mounting up against you. Even challenging the mind to question the heart.

Volume Two

If you wonder, "Did I ask for this? Why bother? This is too much. This is not my passion. This is pitiful. Give up!" These challenge questions and others may be present. Be armed with the strong belt of truth, the breastplate of His approval, and righteousness! You have feet shod (or shoes) with the readiness to speak the Gospel of peace. This enables you to hold up your shield of faith confidently. Being saved, you protect your head with the helmet of salvation. Carry the two-edged sword of the Spirit, God's word. Read, recite, and apply it to your inner me and to defeat the enemy. It is a double-edged sword. See? We are still in the fight. It is spiritual, a fixed fight!

As I reflect upon my life, it seems to unfold into many precious seasons. Some were embarrassing and full of error. Others rendered a plethora of happiness, success, and experience. It was sprinkled with maturity, growth, and setbacks. These experiences comprise our life seasons full of struggles and success. The greater the fight, the greater the results. These results will help you grow. They make you effective at what you do and are called to become! Kingdom will test you, try you, and then prove you!

I Made It Out

In January 2019, at the California International Music Products Association (NAMM) show. I enjoyed great success that year. Our showcase was labeled groundbreaking. Celebrating and sick, I never realized I was in a fight for my life. I could not sleep; my legs and feet were swelling rapidly. I was in tremendous pain. I had shortness of breath. My urine was as dark orange. I was scared, but in California. I had to get home. I made it back East.

The following day and a day after, I was in the hospital. The doctors were amazed! They asked how I even made the five-hour flight home. I said, "God." They nodded, but then said, "Sir, you have an irregular heartbeat. You are full of fluid and your body is not disposing its carbon dioxide. When is the last time you slept?" They whisked me away and performed all sorts of tests until I was sleepy. I was in the Intensive Care Unit (ICU).

About 36 hours later, I woke up with a machine wrapped around my face. I was screaming for them to get it off! Then, I realized that in just 36 hours God turned away death. He guided those doctors, miraculously released the fluids, dismissed the carbon dioxide, and jump-started my heart. My oxygen levels began to regulate. I was living II Corinthians 12:9, His strength was made perfect in my weakness!

I give all honor to God! It is His glory that I worship. I give Him praise daily for total healing and deliverance. The reality of my sickness began my healing process, renewing my desire to live again. I am willing to fight to be healthy and change bad habits to live well. Regardless of doubt, failures, or mistakes I am going to fight.

As a witness, I can testify God will make it right if you just stay in the fight. Follow His instruction manual, The Holy Bible. I left out the years of depression. My weight issues, my separation from my wife and my family. My immobility and lack of effort were contributing factors. The fact is, I was disconnected spiritually, and I no longer had on His full armor. I was not prophetic. I was pathetic. My life was not ministry. It was motivated by industry. I was not sensitive to His word; I got comfortable with my own. I did not want to pray, and I would not fast. But I was in church all the time, just 'doing church'.

It was sad! The attack was mental, physical, spiritual, and self-inflicted all because of disobedience. I was 'sin sick'. But my deliverance report is found in Galatians 2:20, *"I'm crucified with Christ, nevertheless I live, yet not I, but Christ liveth in me and the life which I now live in the flesh I live by faith of the Son of God who loved me, and gave himself for me."* Because Christ fixed it, I am still in the fight!

-Elder Jeff Davis

Volume Two

CHAPTER 6: HE WILL NEVER FORSAKE ME

Volume Two

Hebrews 13:5 expresses one of the most comforting promises of scripture, *"...[God] will never leave or forsake you."* It is a blessing to know God is ever present. He is unwilling to abandon or leave us without the power of His presence. Certainly, this connotation is at the heart of the scripture. It is not necessarily at the heart of what it means to forsake.

To forsake is one of the most fluid words of scriptural language. It goes well beyond simply departing from something or someone. Its simplest meaning could indeed mean to depart. The writer intends to convey a subtle yet separate idea between leaving and forsaking. That is why he used both words. Therefore, to forsake carries a different sentiment and was used to add depth to God's commitment toward us.

To leave is connected to the action of departing or going away from something or someone. To forsake, takes into consideration both departing and going away from something or someone. One must remain in a condition after the departure from those which are usually a negative or adversarial. Forsaking goes far beyond just leaving and it is more likened to abandonment or desertion.

Abandonment brings feelings of helplessness, emptiness, and loneliness. It heightens despair and intensifies any misery life brings your way. Abandonment leaves one with the feeling of being left in a situation with no resolution. After you have exhausted your wisdom, tapped your resources, and the worse reality possible is beginning to settle in. No help is on the way.

There are emotions one experiences just before loss. Before a loved one expires. There is nothing left for you to do. Before the mortgage company takes the keys to the house, you have no remaining resources to stop them. A spouse says they are leaving, and you cannot change their heart. To feel abandoned is having the hollowed void associated with not knowing what to do next.

The idea, the writer is expressing life goes awry. Maybe off centered, or even in dire straits and you have no answers. God would never even consider leaving you alone in such a condition. Absolutely not! In fact, God is aware that these are the moments you need Him the most.

Forsake also carries an inference of renunciation and betrayal. To forsake is also to formally reject something, mainly one's responsibility an idea, a promise or oath. The beauty of God's love toward us is that it inspires His commitment to the idea He had concerning your life. Each promise that He made to you, the oath He swore by His own name to be there with you.

God understands that if He were to ever forsake you, it would erode your trust in Him and destroy any chance at true intimacy with you. God never intends to betray your trust. He will never walk away and leave you. Nothing could ever convince Him to change His heart about it.

God cannot be turned off by your life, your mistakes, or your current situation. He will not be shy asserting His presence in your life, even in your worst situations. In fact, Psalm 46:1 says He is, *"...a very present help in times of trouble."* He is not just near. He is active in helping with the solution to your troubles.

Volume Two

Regardless of actions you have done, been involved in, or are currently involved in God's steadfast promise stands. He simply and absolutely refuses to walk off and force you to fend for yourself. You cannot push Him away or make Him so angry and disappointed in you that He would walk away. God has made a promise. For our benefit, He keeps His promises. He will not be abandoned, reject, refuse, or betray you. In short, God will never forsake you.

Take this simple yet profound promise and be encouraged. Allow it to fill you with hope. During steady times let it inspire gratitude and in difficult times, faith. God is for you and is working with you to make you more like Him. You are not doing it alone, He is not going to leave, nor forsake you. *"...For he himself has said, 'I will never leave you nor forsake you."* (Hebrews 13:5)

-Dr. Terrell Fletcher

CHAPTER 7: YOUR HIGHER WAYS

Volume Two

When we discuss God's way, we must consider His 'higher ways'. I suggest we investigate the spirit of healing. First, identify the affliction and why it requires healing. It must be a mission. Whether pain manifests as physical, emotional, or mental pain, determine in your mind you want to be healed. Sometimes there is no cure, answer, alternative treatment, or antidote to heal physical and mental pains. There is something that can heal us emotionally, the Spirit. If that is your desire and hope.

I want to share my story with you about how the Spirit of healing helped me. I knew my father-in-law since I was nine years old. I knew him before I knew his family. I knew him from my experiences of performing in a professional choir. Only, I knew him from a distance. I knew his personality. I knew him from 30,000 feet away.

When he became my father-in-law, my perspective gradually decreased from 30,000 to 10,000 feet. Then 10,000 became 5,000 feet. Eventually 5,000 became 1,000 feet. We remained at a 1,000 feet distance. We did not have an extremely close relationship.

Volume Two

As I reflect, it may be because he did not have his own relationship with his father. This man knew how to communicate with a crowd but was challenged on a more personal level. Often, he referred to me as 'my daughter's husband' instead of as his son-in-law. I never took it personally and I never judged him. I knew I had to look at him from a different perspective. I examined myself too. I understood his predicament. He did not know either of his parents. I understood not having a father. I respected, him as one older and wiser in a variety of areas. I realized; I may have more sensitivity to communicate on a more personal level than he.

I wanted to be included in his business deals and meetings. I was at the age where I could be. Instead, my father-in-law, would invite others, not me. I could not figure it out. Eventually, I forsook the desire and kept it to myself. It became a source of pain. When you hold a position as a father or father-in-law, there are responsibilities and obligations. I did not know how to approach the situation. Maybe all the situation required was for me to make him aware. Instead, I left it alone.

My father-in-law was remarkably successful. Often, he referred to me and my education as a 'poverty professional'. I do not think he meant any harm. Internally, it created a gap, between us. My father-in-law was also a popular and successful pastor. Many times, I wanted to help him in his church and life. I knew of certain ways to help. I stopped extending myself to him because it was never embraced.

From my perspective, there appeared to be no value in what I could offer to my father-in-law. I did not pursue because, I wanted to be validated. My mission was to find areas to affirm me, my work. Men and women who grow up without their fathers are either overachievers or underachievers. They seek validation. When it is not received, they will either fight or flight, forsake the task. Sometimes you may attempt both actions. By overachieving on certain aspects of their life for a period and underachieving on others.

I always respected my father-in-law and included him on any project on which I worked. I wondered why I was not invited to contribute to his work. He would invite someone possibly lacking the skill set, network connections, or knowledge base to perform the task.

Volume Two

This was from my perspective, what I thought and felt. In truth, they could have been equipped to execute his plans correctly.

When my wife and I moved to Hawaii, the physical distance made the estrangement even more profound. I did not have to confront the thoughts and feelings of rejection anymore. The truth of the matter is, I should have dealt with those emotions from the beginning. But I did not know how. My foundation did not include skills either. We were men lacking a certain foundational component. It took a crisis to bring healing.

Crisis came when my father-in-law became ill. I knew my wife needed to go home to Florida to be with her parents. At that point, I decided to commute between Florida and Hawaii every two weeks. The situation grew direr. We realized, while his family loved and cared for him, I was the best equipped to aid. I had to choose. Would I sacrifice for someone who called me a 'poverty professional' and neglected to include me? During his time of illness, I had to choose to care completely or partially. As a caregiver, you choose.

One day on the way to the hospital, my father-in-law asked me if I was going to 'stick with him' through his illness. During the ride, he also told me he wanted to write a book. I thought it would be good for his mental health. He was a prolific songwriter. He already authored several books. He asked me and other family members to write an excerpt in his book. I wrote about the spirit of healing.

He presented my excerpt to his publisher. The publisher did not want to include my contribution. He felt it was a separate book. It did not flow with the rest of the content. He encouraged me to write my own book. This book, "I Made It Out" you hold, is personally inspirational. Up close and personal, I witnessed how my father-in-law was trapped between truth and facts on so many levels. Despite him being a great orator, businessman, and family provider, he too was trapped. Sometimes, we are all caught between our ways and God's way. Allow the Lord's way to prevail.

I returned to Hawaii to conduct a training. I remember when I arrived in my hotel room, it was still daylight. After gazing at the Pacific Ocean, I went inside. I got down on my knees and asked God to heal me. I remembered, someone shared with me about fire types. The person taught, there were three types of fire. A yellow heat can burn rubber. Blue heat is enough to burn steel. White heat is pure heat.

I asked God to give me 'white heat'. I desired to give all and not be consumed by what I thought I could not control. I lacked communication skills, unknowingly. I asked God to grant me a spirit of healing, not just for my father-in-law, but for me to bless others. I prayed for God my own father. I wanted to forgive him for abusing my mom.

I needed 'white heat.' I knew my biological father kicked my mom in the stomach while she was carrying me. It was an attempt to abort me. I continued to ask God for 'white heat' to give me pure joy and love. The kind of joy and love that could make my spirit pure. While I am not perfect, I do want to be clean and pure. Now, understand this 'white heat' purification is metaphoric, not actual.

As I talk about the spirit of healing, my pursuit is to be clean, not perfect. My godfather and great friend, D.J. Rogers, wrote the song, "I Just Want to be Clean Inside." I may not be perfect on the outside. I never will be. But I must get clean. This is a daily pursuit. I encourage you to get to clean.

You must get into an emotional state. Be truthful and transparent with yourself about the pains, joys, and fight in that space. Do not lie about your state, instead share, and communicate. Believe, it is not all bad. This is an aspect of your life. Whether you were molested as a child, abused as an adult, lied to, or misunderstood; find your freedom in the spirit of healing.

This is the difference between your ways and God's higher ways. This is where the spirit of healing exists. If you do not deal with the process, the spirit of healing will not show up. You will always have that emptiness and a void. Your story may not be like mine. We all have issues and pain.

Look for God's higher ways. I hope you gain insight on the Lord's higher ways for your life. I hope you allow yourself to be vulnerable. I want you to dream, pursue your passions, and thrive. I

Volume Two

want you to have grace for yourself as you seek out God's ways. I want you to take the spirit of healing with you always.

If you start to drift back into old patterns, I pray you will pick up this book and read it again. You never know what you will find the second or third time around. Something may resonate with you. You may be awakened to new possibilities. Walk in your freedom. Bask in the knowledge that every day you are learning to love yourself more and more.

-Elder Leven Wilson

CHAPTER 8: MOVING ON

Volume Two

One of the most challenging experiences in the human journey is moving forward after one has suffered a great loss. It can be frightening to move on to the next. Many never had confidence that extreme greatness existed or was planned for their lives. Many live with just enough and never quite enough. This mentality that must be broken. From the day you were born, there was a promise made over your life.

God does not create us just to exist. He creates us to make a difference. Here becomes the war that resides within. The enemy knows your purpose, as God's creation. He tries to do everything possible to either divert you from functioning in your purpose. Or he attempts to pollute you from having a pure heart to fulfill your assignment given by the Creator.

In the book of Genesis, the Bible introduces us to Joseph. Joseph was the son of Jacob. From the day of Joseph's birth, Jacob showed tremendous affection and love for his son. He set aside space and time to really express his affection for this son. He surrounded him with items that highlighted and separated him from his other siblings.

His brothers envied the public display of care their father consistently showed towards their younger brother. Just like Joseph, some things you suffer, have nothing to do with you. They are thrust upon you based on circumstances. Others will do things to you simply because they cannot stop something that is already functioning in you. They become angry with you. They may attempt to hurt you to prevent you from functioning or fulfilling your purpose.

We take this hurt and look at it from the standpoint of how others feel about us. This is a dangerous place to be. If you are not careful this can cause you to misdiagnose the relationships and intentions of others. Generally, people do not dislike other people because of a hatred within their heart for the person. They tend to dislike other individuals because of deep hidden jealousy that has been discovered due to a favorable condition one has been awarded.

Joseph's brothers could not do anything about the favor their father was demonstrating. So, they took it out on their younger brother Joseph taught us how to deal with unfair circumstances. He showed us, no matter how difficult or how challenging the circumstance maybe, we must be quick to forget and ready to move forward.

There is a danger of staying focused on offenses too long. Focusing on where you were hurt will cause you to create a reality that is false. All of us have dealt with something that allowed us to be injured, disturbed, bothered, or just simply wounded by the display of what came against us. On most occasions, these feelings were inflicted upon us when we were in one of our most pure stages of life.

Joseph's brothers took him and threw him into a pit only to come back and sell him into slavery. The text says, "…and the Lord was with him." In many cases when the Lord is with me it does not feel like it. I can even remember saying, "God if you are for me, why don't you prevent me from even dealing with what I face?" In those moments, we must know the plan of God for our life. It does not allow us to accept defeat in our lives.

Through the process of personal development, Joseph is called to lead people in one of the most challenging times of his land. Like

Volume Two

Joseph, many of us have been privileged to get a sneak peek into our future. This is one of the reasons it is so challenging to deal with the obstacles we face daily. We know there is greater upon us. Can God trust you with highly classified information?

In many cases, we find that God will call us to something that we are not quite capable or conditioned to function in. In this place, God will lead us down a pathway called personal development. Development is necessary for your destiny. Roadblocks, bumps, and bruises are all necessary to mature us into who we shall be. The greatest challenge to development is to stay focused when journeying to the predestined goal.

Whatever did not kill you was designed to develop you. All the challenging moments were totally necessary for the promise God made to you. Embrace your challenges. Walk boldly before the Lord and know that God's hand is upon your life. As believers of Jesus Christ, we are never fighting to win the battle. We are simply fighting not to give up. We trust the process even when we do not understand the totality of the promise. We know that God will strengthen us and bring us to the place He promised.

The Bible tells us, His ways are not our ways, and His thoughts are not our thoughts. God does unusual things to produce supernatural promises. Trust Him in all your ways and lean not to your own understanding. In all your ways acknowledge Him and He shall direct your path. Do not allow the failures of yesterday to be etched into your mental 'Hall of Shame'. Instead, look at every failed place and use it as a steppingstone to move into the direction of the promise. There is so much more ahead, stay focused and know that your labor is not in vain.

-Pastor Derrick L. McRae

Volume Two

CHAPTER 9: LORD, I'M WILLING

Volume Two

When the Lord request an assignment be fulfilled, He is gracious enough to ask, "Who is willing?" This chapter will provide a thought-provoking process concerning willingness to carry out God-given assignments. In Isaiah 6:8, the Lord asked whom He could send. Isaiah responded, *"Here I am; send me."* Isaiah volunteered himself before knowing any conditions and specific details. He understood this meant a great sacrifice. His yes was not predicated on what he may or may not lose.

When you are aware of the sacrifice, you are not afraid of surrendering. Isaiah being willing to fulfill his assignment from God put him in an uncomfortable place. Isaiah was already a prophet speaking to the people. In this defining moment he became more willing and submitted to the voice of God. Isaiah was required to pray, give correction, and deliver the Lord's word to the people whether they liked it or not.

This may have caused him to be judged or even disliked. However, Isaiah was not seeking favor from the people. He was obedient to the voice of God. We may desire approval from our peers.

Volume Two

Favor will come at a greater honor from God. First, we must be willing to follow through with our commission from Him.

A valuable lesson Isaiah's life teaches is that our willingness must be developed through our desire to please God. This causes us to complete our assignments regardless of our personal agendas and comfort. God revealing our purpose and path does not mean He will not challenge us. Our mindset and sensitivity to the needs of the kingdom must change. Willingness is not conditional, but unconditional. As Isaiah, we all experience a defining moment. We should declare, "Lord! I'm willing." To develop a willing mindset, you will need the 'three A's': availability, arrangement, and ambulation.

The Three A's:

Availability is the quality to be used or obtained. It is the freedom to perform something with persistence to see it through to completion. Being available is obedience and submission to an assignment without hesitation. After you make yourself completely available, you are then able to organize an arrangement.

To arrange is to plan or prepare for the future. Everything we do requires proper preparation. If you are not prepared to prosper, you will not. Arrangements must align with an end goal. When you are not willing to make the necessary changes, you cannot complete a task.

Finally, to ambulate is to move forward. The final step in your willingness to your assignment is to walk in it and move forward. You can say yes, be available, and make the proper arrangements. If you do not resolve to move forward and complete it, you will not.

Being called to pastor required me to prioritize the 'Three A's' to fulfill the assignment I accepted. I told God I was willing. Personally, the 'Three A's' looked different in my journey. Availability was a huge element of sacrifice for me. Constantly, I had to be willing to forgo something to fulfill my assignment. Previous commitments had to be altered for me to be available, as I promised God. My role in others' lives had to change due to the role I was serving as a pastor.

Being available to God often means becoming unavailable to people. Being available to God also means sacrificing things that do not align with your assignment. After I changed my availability, my arrangement was preset. I prepared for all I was to which I was to receive access. What an assignment comes strength, favor, information, and a new level in understanding your call.

This is a new level of power. Anyone who obtains this power must be disciplined. Discipline comes with preparation. With my arrangement, I knew I had to conquer my highest form of preparation. I had to prepare more than I ever to get where I had never been. I would have to educate, lead, and guide people. My availability and arrangement pushed me to say, "Lord, I'm willing."

Often when fulfilling the next level of our assignment, we attempt to lead as the leader which proceeded us. My leadership had to be unique and tailored to those following me, as I followed Christ. A different approach does not mean I did not respect the amazing examples before me. It simply meant God's kingdom needed diversity. I knew while God gave me a similar calling, He would not give me the same instructions for the same results. If He called me, it was because He needed who I was, my authenticity.

I began doing research to support my willingness. Research was incredibly significant. I wanted to make sure I was being true to myself by not mocking those before me. I took pride in research. It was my way of showing God I took His call seriously. It was my goal to handle His people responsibly. Research allowed me to make my willingness plain. I knew exactly what I wanted ministry to be.

My arrangement dealt significantly with people. Not necessarily how to handle people but how to educate and lead them. I made it my mission to research and reach out. I would contact people and educate them. I was very intentional with whom I educated and contacted.

I believed God intentionally put people in place that were willing to help me carry out my assignment. He knew who was meant to walk this journey with me, follow me, and learn from me. I targeted those people in my process of educating through arrangement. If people could not identify the plan God gave me, they would not respect the assignment or acknowledge my call.

Volume Two

The knowledge I provided was based on what we needed as a team. Identifying who is a part of your team is identifying other willing vessels; those who will also submit to the call as you did. I kept in my forefront; my willingness was not dependent upon others' participation. It was based on my consistent surrender. I became so focused on the assignment that it did not matter who stayed or left. My goal was to inspire and promote the willingness in those who remained.

Fulfilling my assignment would be done by any means necessary. I had to realize others accompanying me may have their own assignment with different instructions. I came to the realization I had to fulfill my mission until the end, regardless of the commitment of others. I knew my instructions. They were to be prioritized and completed. I was in a state of ambulation, moving forward regardless of circumstances. Availability and arrangement prepared me to ambulate. It took all the necessary discipline to keep moving forward.

> In this moment I became more like Abraham in Genesis 12:1-3. *"The Lord had said to Abram, Go from your country, your people and your father's household to the land I will show you. I will make you into a great nation, and I will bless you; I will make your name great, and you will be a blessing. I will bless those who bless you,*

and whoever curses you I will curse; and all peoples on earth will be blessed through you."

I departed from everything I knew, my home. I completely committed to pastoring and gained favor from my obedience. God made me a promise based on my obedience. I took on my own congregation. I began leading God's people the way He called me to lead.

Distractions came in all areas: financial and manpower. Any distraction you can name, it can and most likely will happen. Distractions taught me, no matter how much the method may change, follow the instructions in fulfilling your assignment. The key thing to distraction is identifying it as such. You cannot handle a distraction with diligence. You need the power to see it is indeed a distraction.

As willing vessels our vulnerability, interest, and desires put us in denial about what may be a distraction for us. When we refocus on our assignment, we can cast these cares aside. In identifying the distraction, have the integrity to call it a hindrance or obstacle. Realize it is a problem. You will be more likely to want to eliminate it.

Realize though it is a desire you once had, a vulnerability or interest; it is not a priority. Anything that is not a priority when you have a goal in mind, is a distraction. Utilize the 'three A's': availability, arrangement, and ambulation. They are the keys to you truly being a willing vessel. Respond to God's call. Say, "Lord, I'm willing."

- Pastor Darrell Blair

CHAPTER 10: I'M YET CONFIDENT

Volume Two

"...[A]nd David inquired of the Lord saying, Shall I pursue after this troop? Shall I overtake them? And he answered him, Pursue: for thou shalt surely overtake them, and without fail recover all." 1 Samuel 30:8

A thermometer assesses the temperature in a place or an area. It does not change anything in the area. It only registers the present temperature. A thermostat sets the temperature for an environment. It regulates the surroundings and changes them when they need to be adjusted. Our goal in life should be to live with a 'thermostat mentality' and not a thermometer one. A thermometer mentality only seeks to define what exists. A thermostat mentality sets the temperature despite the present. In the passage David used this moment to view his circumstance from a thermostat perspective.

David and his army men returned from a victorious battle. Their families were captured, and their homes burned down. Can you imagine how they felt? Initially, the men thought of stoning David. They believed if they had been home, they would have defended their households. David was at a point of great distress. As David and the men wept for the loss of their families and homes. While David was weeping, his army's resentment grew. They fought in support of David and left their homeland vulnerable. He had to encourage himself in the Lord. He could have run away or fought his own army.

Instead, David chose to improve his environment despite the present situation. There was no need to measure the climate, he needed to change the climate. Psalms 27:1-3 reveals David's confidence in the Lord.

> *"The Lord is my light and my salvation; whom shall I fear? The Lord is the strength of my life; of whom shall I be afraid? When the wicked, even mine enemies and my foes, came upon me to eat up my flesh, they stumbled and fell. Though an host should encamp against me, my heart shall not fear: though war should rise against me, in this will I be confident."*

The confidence David comes from how he esteems his own life. David is not ignoring his situation, hoping that it goes away. He has confidence despite the situation, he has faith. The land was scorched from fire at the hands of his enemies. No house was left standing. Their families were taken captive and carried off to another land.

In the face of this atrocity, David was able to be strong because he believed the enemy did not kill any of the captured. They were taken against their will, but David believed they were still alive unharmed. In life, we can be distracted by our circumstances. We can miss the fact; we are still alive. The soldiers in David's army were weeping. But David believed, if there is still life there is still hope.

In life, you may encounter an enemy, dealing with things beyond your control. Our powerful and protective God will give you the grace to live through it. You may wonder if your current circumstance will ever come to an end. You may be thinking this is your end. I want to encourage you to remember, you still have life. The favor and blessings of God are not on a place. They are on you. Everywhere you go, carry that favor on your life. Remain confident, God is your light and your salvation.

In this time of despair, David seeks the Lord for a strategy. To encourage himself, seeking the Lord was the best way to do it. He did not just pray a general prayer. He requested a strategy to produce results. There is no purpose in requesting a strategy without confidence it will work.

Volume Two

This can be a place of encouragement. When everyone else is gone and it seems the weight of the world is on your shoulders, seek the Lord. He can give you what no one else could. As David seeks the Lord, he asks for instructions. Then the Lord gave him an answer. Without seeking the Lord, David would not have received the answer.

Often God will allow us to experience a situation to cause us to seek Him for direction. As you move forward toward obtaining your desired goals, it is extremely crucial that you seek the Lord and drown out other opinions. The answer David received provided instruction and inspiration. *"Pursue and you will without fail recover all."*

God gave David the conclusion before he set out to act. This is the benefit of being confident in the Lord. David knew the end of the story while he was still living amid the dilemma. David was confident pursuing. He knew it was going to work in his favor. Not only would he experience victory, but he would not lose anything in the process.

All you have read, prayed, and thought about will strengthen you for the shifting taking place in your life. As God said to David, I also

I Made It Out

say to you, "You will overcome without failure. Your life was saved and purposed for success." You may experience some difficulties and obstacles. But be encouraged and know with confidence that you will not fail. Do not waste another moment wondering if you will accomplish your goal. Failure is not an option. Shift your mind, change your words and actions. Make this declaration, "I am yet confident! I made it out, alright!"

-Minister Daniel Sutton

Volume Two

CHAPTER 11: HE PREPARED ME

Volume Two

I Made It Out

During the 1960s, one of my favorite weekly television program was "Mission Impossible." It was about a group of highly trained operatives all experts in their fields. They would be given seemingly 'impossible' espionage missions to accomplish. Their highly classified super-secret assignment usually involved overthrowing a sinister foreign government or regime. The target was a threat to the interest of the free world.

Their missions were so secret and sensitive. No one in law enforcement or government could know about the existence of their unit or the mission. The given assignment always arrived by message on a self-destructing tape recorder. On the tape the 'particulars' or details of the mission were revealed. The mission would always be based on one condition, "If you choose to accept it…" But it ended with a warning, "If you or any member of the team is caught their mission would be disavowed." This caution emphasized the fact that this indeed was an 'impossible mission'.

When you consider the word 'impossible,' it is a subtle play on words. The missions were never impossible. However, the word

Volume Two

impossible implied it was fraught with dangers making the assignment precarious. Each mission would present new circumstances and challenges. It caused the unit to be stretched beyond their limits and taken beyond their boundaries.

The team had to overcome obstacles and perils, both seen and unseen to accomplish the task. Each clandestine mission presented its own 'impossible circumstances.' Because the team possessed a skill sets and were battle tested through experience, they were well equipped. They could turn the impossible into possible. They came prepared to overcome and win.

Throughout the seasons of our life, God gives us assignments. He has prepared us to accomplish each one. How many times have we said, "God, I cannot handle this situation, I cannot do this task! God, I don't want this assignment!" Despite our complaining and hesitation, God says, "I prepared you. You will not only make it through, but you will win!"

When the Lord is preparing us, we cannot see the purpose in the process. We do not even know we are being prepared. From our perspective, the vicissitudes of life seem to be one string of arbitrary events. Each trial and test may seem impossible and insurmountable. Times we cannot reconcile nor find our own way out.

Rest assured; challenges are preparation for your God-given assignment. God prepared specific challenges to shape you into the person He called you to be. Whether you understand it or not, you are being conditioned to be more than a conqueror through Christ that loves us.

> Ephesians 3:20 declares, *"Now unto him that is able to do exceeding abundantly above all that we ask or think, according to the power that worketh in us."*

This passage presents us with an interesting dichotomy. It states, God can do that which is totally 'beyond you' based upon that which is working 'within you'. God has worked something great within you. You cannot comprehend it until you work through adversity. Only then can you realize the full potential of the power God has worked within you.

Volume Two

As we traverse this arduous journey called life, we experience all sorts of seemingly unrelated painful circumstances. We often think they are unnecessary. Understand, every one of these trials plays an important part in our preparation and development. Every mountain climbed, detour passed, setup foiled, and setback regained is God working it out for your good. Your steps have been divinely arranged and ordered by the Lord.

Nothing you go through, shall overtake. The Lord has prepared you for His purpose in glory. God has a mission. It is possible and for you. The apostle Paul encapsulates God's divine preparation process when he informs us, *"For you are God's workmanship created in Christ Jesus unto good works, that he has before ordained that we should walk in them."* (Ephesians 2:10).

In trials, the imperfections of impossibility are burned off. Possibility is forged and tempered. It is in the 'fire' where God works his best in us. Through the flames of adversity, in the furnace of affliction, emerges a new creation. From a transformed heart come a beautiful testimony, rhythmic words of worship, and powerful praise flow. We offer to God the fruit of our lips. We are truly transformed into God's masterpiece.

Adversity allows the Lord to temper our faith and teach us how to trust Him. We then walk into the reality that, *"Faith is the substance of things hope for and the evidence of things not seen."* (Hebrews 11:1). In the valley of despair, we learn to wait on the Lord, to walk by faith and not by sight.

> *"Dear friends, do not be surprised at the fiery ordeal that has come on you to test you, as though something strange were happening to you. But rejoice inasmuch as you participate in the sufferings of Christ, so that you may be overjoyed when his glory is revealed."* (1 Peter 4:12-13, NIV).

God does not forsake us but causes our mistakes to work together for our good. Our trials are not coincidental arbitrary sets of happenstances. There is a purpose in the pain and power in the plan of God to see you through. By this, you are delivered, and God gets the glory. Tests are intentional and uniquely designed to strengthen our most holy faith.

We must overcome the one impossibility that exist between God and us, unbelief. *"Without faith it is impossible to please God."*

(Hebrews 11:6a). Unbelief is hostile to faith. In Matthew 17:20-21 the Lord said, *"Truly I tell you, if you have faith as small as a mustard seed, you can say to this mountain, 'Move from here to there,' and it will move. Nothing will be impossible for you."*

Only through faith can the impossible become possible. We serve an all-powerful God. With Him, nothing is impossible. For God to transport from the grips of impossible to the liberty of possible, God must prepare you. He has prepared me to live a victorious life because, *"I can do all things through Christ that strengthens me."* (Philippians 4:13). He prepared me to trust Him. He prepared me to praise Him. He prepared me to love Him. He prepared me to serve Him. No matter what shall come your way, through its all, He prepared.

-Dr. Derrick J. Hughes

CHAPTER 12: LIVE AGAIN

Volume Two

I Made It Out

On a cold rainy day in 1975, I was so overwhelmingly depressed, at a breaking point. Alone again, I cried looking for relief. I could not figure out what I needed. The battle I was dealing with was beyond my immature age of 14. Coming of age was not easy for me. I had strong family, friends, and as I thought, happiness. My life was about to change forever. I walked in depression.

A slump of despair manifested itself as a concealed mask. I had no desire to be with family nor friends. I stayed to myself from the age of 11, in my room. Living in the St. Nicholas Projects of Harlem, New York back in the 1970's was not easy. Compulsive crime, drugs, and widespread poverty was at an all-time high.

Ghetto living had a way of breaking down a mind each day unwittingly. I became lonely and absent from everything. I wanted and needed what I came to realize now was an escape. Through the eyes of the beholder, seeing death and hearing gun shots daily was culturally considered normal. Deviant behavior established parameters that was measured as natural. Seemingly accepted, the pain either drew you in or cried out. I tried to escape with sports, joining football and basketball teams. Nothing helped my soul searching.

My first experience with drugs was at the tender age of 11. My friend had a brother, who in the projects had an alias. He was known as 'Crazy"' He earned this name because he did so many drugs daily. Often, he would do outlandish, crazy, and 'bugged out' things. My friend took his brother's marijuana joints. We stole a car, rolled up the car windows, and lit the joints. We got so high and hungry at the same time.

The 'munchies' exposed us to other ailments that increased daily. The 'munchies' and a sweet tooth, dangerous. Looking innocent was our claim to bravery. As we continued to get high, it led to thievery and deceptions. We stole many things, robbed bystanders, and graduated to higher levels of drugs.

The summer of 1972, I had my very first girlfriend and she was very experienced sexually. Later that day, I told my devious partner in crime about my experience. He decided to get a joint from his brother 'Crazy's' stash. We lit that joint almost immediately and became so

I Made It Out

high, we both took off running in different directions with no one chasing us.

The only thing I remember is being stopped by what I thought was at the time was a little person and his taller brother. Unbeknownst to us, 'Crazy' had advanced in his drugging beyond our capability to handle. My friend's brother was crazy for too many strange reasons to count. Angel dust had us tripping like we were as bugged out as 'Crazy' himself.

As time passed, I found new crime partners. They did not do drugs, but they knew how to steal. We would go into the local department store, take tips, and snatch bags. We stole food from kids exiting fast food restaurants. A big pay day was planned. We robbed a store at night. We counted the loot and divided it amongst ourselves evenly.

I was now 14 years old. My life was changing so rapidly. I did not want to hang out with my girlfriend or friends. I remember my girl calling me outside of our fourth-floor apartment window asking me to come outside. She said, "If you can't come outside then I am going to find another boyfriend." I said, "Ok," and went back inside. My mother asked me on several occasions why I did not want to go outside. I told her repeatedly, "I did not have the desire to anymore." The summer of 1974 ended.

My day of change came a few months later. Fall bringing a seasonal change. So was my life. A cold rain was slowly coming down. A new partner in sinful thoughts began its troubles. I heard, "Kill yourself." It was so loud and meaningful to my young mind. Full of depression, loneliness, and overwhelming sadness, I started walking in the rain.

This new partner did not talk much. But when he did, he made me feel so much more miserable and depressed. Suicide was my new real friend. My suicidal journey led me towards a bridge in Harlem on 145th Street. I stared across a river of hopelessness. I lifted my little leg up and I began to lift my other.

I Made It Out

A man approached me. Asking no questions, he pulled me up and away from the bridge of my foreseen death. He walked the opposite way across the bridge. I began to walk back in the direction from which I came. I did not know what to make of it. I just knew within myself I did not want to die.

Unfortunately, for many battling depressions this is not always the case. Prevention starts with signs. Depression without aide or help cannot be resolved with a shout or only prayer. It takes knowledgeable counsel and spiritual advice to help. The remedy for me was deliverance.

Symptoms of suicidal thoughts:

- Wanting to be alone and isolated
- Unhappy conversations
- Dressed untidy
- Loss of weight and appetite
- Behavioral change in attitude
- Conversations about killing or hurting themselves

My life changed forever after I walked back across the 145th Street Bridge in Harlem. The following year on August 15, 1975, I made it out. I walked back across that same bridge in the same direction as that man. I later learned it to have been an angel. He pulled me away.

Volume Two

Under a big gospel tent, I accepted Jesus Christ as my Lord and Savior. God pulled me off the edge. He helped me understand Christ deliverance. I dedicated my livelihood to share the Gospel of Jesus Christ ever since. "Yes, I made it out alright!"

-Bishop Ezekiel Newton

CHAPTER 13: KNOW YOUR STORY

Volume Two

I Made It Out

Through the years, I had the pleasure of meeting several talented and successful people. They included fellow writers, performing artists, educators, politicians, businesspeople, and entrepreneurs. As one would imagine, we did not always agree on every topic. However, consistently I found a common ground with my contemporaries. It was about reconciling the past. It is required to move toward into a more successful future. I prefer calling it, "Looking back, to move forward."

It is imperative for our spiritual, emotional, and intellectual growth that we take an honest look at our past, assess our experiences. Consider both the good and bad. Focus on your earliest memories. Those experiences contribute the most with shaping who we are today. Their impact is greater than our education, career experiences, or any other factor. We all have stories to tell. By reflecting on our earliest recollections, we can move forward to a clearer perception of others and ourselves.

> Throughout the scriptures we are reminded that God never intended for us live as though yesterday never existed. Deuteronomy 4:9 encourages us to recall our experiences. It states how doing so benefits future generations. *"Only give heed to*

> *yourself and keep your soul diligently, so that you do not forget the things which your eyes have seen and they do not depart from your heart all the days of your life; but make them known to your sons and your grandsons."*

Deuteronomy 32:7 further suggests we ask our parents and elders to share with us what they know of the generations before us. *"Remember the days of old, consider the years of all generations. Ask your father, and he will inform you, your elders, and they will tell you."*

I was never comfortable with reflecting on past experiences. I felt I was somehow dishonoring God by not laying aside the old man (Ephesians 4:22). I learned to take stock of past experiences. I studied them as I would a carefully crafted novel. It helped me renew the spirit of my mind and put on the new man (Ephesians 4:23-24) as God instructs us.

I am convinced, the 'never look back, keep your eyes on the prize' philosophy is based in part on Genesis 19:26. It describes Lot's wife turning back to look upon the destruction of Sodom and Gomorrah. *"But his wife, from behind him, looked back, and she became a pillar of salt."* This story is used as a cautionary tale for anyone who focuses more on revisiting their past. Instead they are instructed to keep their eyes facing forward and fixed on the future.

Unfortunately, such a narrow interpretation of the story really misses a critical point. A more thorough analysis of the story would allow us to see that the story of Lot's wife turning into a pillar of salt is representative of her longing to return to a life of sin (imbalance). The way of life God was allowing her to escape, was that for which she longed. Longing for a life that is morally and spiritually bankrupt is quite different than utilizing God's gift of reflection. Reflecting can assist you in having more clarity of thought regarding your future.

Furthermore, learn from the experiences of the generations that preceded you as the scriptures encourage in Deuteronomy. This is entirely different from what Lot's wife was accused of in Genesis. Oversimplification of a complex story is a major contributor to teaching a doctrine that misleads those who would benefit from an honest account of their past.

Leaders Understand the Power of Knowing their Story:

Volume Two

> Dr. William W. Wilmot and Dr. Joyce L. Hocker share, "Our personal history in our families of origin will have a big impact on what we choose to do with our lives. Our personal history includes all our interactions with others up to the present. What we experience as a preschooler, in school, with friends on the playground, and in all our adult exchanges - influences our expectations."

For as long as I can remember, I was fascinated with the life of social reformer and abolitionist, Frederick Douglass. Douglass' life is a case study in reconciling past experiences. He simultaneously utilized those past experiences to move toward a more successful future. Born a slave in February 1818, Douglas would rise to international acclaim as an abolitionist while the masses of black people were enslaved. Douglass' was able to accomplish so much when so many variables were against him. It came from his personal commitment to truth and a broadening awareness.

A newspaper reporting on a lecture that Douglass gave in 1844, wrote that many people in the audience refused to believe his stories. A quote from the newspaper read: "How a man, only six years out of bondage, and who had never gone to school could speak with such eloquence - with such precision of language and power of thought - they were utterly at a loss to devise."

I am persuaded that Douglass' success as a social reformer, and abolitionist was due in large part to his ability to "...work through the emotional baggage of [his] youth" (Wilmot and Hocker). Douglass was able to make sense of a childhood spent entirely in bondage. But more than that, the record shows Douglass' managed to retell the horrors of the life of a slave. He recounted events so effectively, even those in power were compelled to take notice. We continue to revere Douglass' accomplishments more than a century after his death.

<u>Sankofa</u>

We must go back and reclaim our past so we can move forward; so, we understand why and how we came to be who we are today

It is strange how easy it is to forget those who sacrificed themselves than was ever expected. For me, it was a little old lady. I remember her as 'Miss. Vallie'. When I was three years old until I was school age, she provided me with the love, guidance, and nurturing. My mother worked and my older siblings attended school. Miss. Vallie would watch me. She was not a babysitter, nanny, or tutor.

Volume Two

Miss. Vallie was a nice older lady who was charged with keeping me when no one else could. I am quite sure mother never paid her more than a couple of dollars a week. It is entirely possible my mother never paid her anything at all. The run-down wood-frame house in which Miss. Vallie lived became an informal training ground of sorts. It is where I learned to mind my manners, respect my elders, and get along with others.

I remember Miss. Vallie used to wash my face each day. She used the same raggedy cloth she used to wash her dishes. Smelling like a stale dishrag was a small price to pay for the care. Miss. Vallie taught me right from wrong and the 'three R's'. Most importantly, she instilled the belief that I could do anything to which I put my mind. At the age of four, I could read, write a complete sentence, add, subtract, and even multiply by two. I was no genius. I was just a kid blessed to be in the company of a little old lady who cared.

A few years later, my Mother took me to visit Miss. Vallie. She appeared even older than I remembered. The tattered little book from which I first learned to read still sat on the mantel. A dishcloth like the

I Made It Out

one used to scrub my face, lay neatly folded on the edge of the kitchen sink. I smiled to myself. I thought about how good it felt to visit the home of the little old lady who gave me more than I could ever give to her in return.

When I started high school, I stopped visiting Miss. Vallie. I suppose like many teenagers I began to get caught up in my own little world. A few years ago, I thought of Miss. Vallie; her selflessness and all she gave to me. I tried to recall Miss. Vallie as she looked when I was a child. But the images I conjured up were vague and distorted. This woman who gifted me with the ability to read and write. The one whom taught me to dream beyond what I could see was now a distorted and vague memory. I was heartbroken.

-Pastor Kelvin De'Marcus Allen

Volume Two

CHAPTER 14: ONE YES AWAY

Volume Two

I Made It Out

Life has a way of bringing us to deciding moments and moments of truth. At this juncture, your decision will direct the trajectory of your life. Locked up in your decision is your destiny. One right move can be the key to light and one wrong move can be the gateway to darkness.

Prior to his crucifixion, Jesus was in the Garden of Gethsemane. Gethsemane is the place at the foot of the Mount of Olives where the oil press was located. It is the place of the pressing out of the juice of the olive. It is where the oil is extracted. The essence of the olive is 'pulled out'. Gethsemane is the place that reveals true character. The pressing in life we experience was never designed to kill us. It was designed to reveal our nature. Gethsemane reveals whether we believe all we have taught and preached about God.

We want to follow God many times for the 'fishes and the loaves'. We want to see him work miracles. There is a place in your following that you come to understand, it costs you more than your time, effort, and energy. It requires your full submission to the will of the

Father. In a defining moment, you must agree with God over yourself. God requires a yes when you want to give him a no.

There are three things that your yes will require of you. First, your yes will require your solitude. Jesus was subject to intense sorrow and agony. He experienced disconnection from the Heavenly Father and disconnection from his earthly mother. There was to experience much pain. He looked at the Father and asked, "If there is any other way to get around this, let this cup pass from me."

Second, a yes requires separation. Your surrender becomes the line of demarcation between what you want and what God wants for you. Jesus says in St. Luke 22:42 (KJV), "[N]evertheless not my will, but thine, be done." We may lose friends, positions, and self-identity. But we must come to the place to the same submission as Christ. Jesus knew that he would experience pain, suffering, tears, and emotional trials.

His disciples failed to stand with him in prayer in his most crucial moment. Perhaps you made assumptions about who should assist you. The place of your yes is where you move on from people whom you thought would support you.

> Hebrews 12:2 reminds, *"Looking unto Jesus the author and finisher of our faith; who for the joy that was set before him endured the cross, despising the shame, and is set down at the right hand of the throne of God."*

Joy is waiting on you. But it is locked up in your yes. You can experience the best days of your life. You must give God a yes. Your yes is a place of surrender. If we trust God, the thing that is so painful will lead us to a place of fulfillment. You are on your way to fulfillment. You are one yes away.

Your yes is your surrender. Surrender is more than singing the hymn, "I Surrender All" at an altar call. It is more than tears or lifting your hands in service and singing, "Yes, Lord". Your yes is bringing your life in to compliance with what the Master has purposed for you. The Hebrew writer said that Jesus saw it as joy set before him.

The 'nevertheless' of Gethsemane is the place of confronting fear of purpose and obedience. Gethsemane is the price of the oil to finish your assignment. I know it may be a difficult place. Finish what you started. This the season that He who begun a good work in you will complete it. God is looking for your yes. Angels appeared in the garden and strengthened Jesus. It may not be what you want, but what God wants for you. Nevertheless says, "I'm tired of depending on flesh." My 'nevertheless' is my unconditional yes.

"Trust the Lord with all your heart and lean not to your own understanding." Proverbs 3:5 (NKJV). You have nothing to prove. You are already accepted by the Beloved. What God has for you is so far beyond what you could ever ask or imagine. Our answer must be 'yes' to whatever God wants. That yes will open a door of deliverance, healing, miracles, signs, wonders, prosperity, and hope.

Whatever you want me to do, my answer is 'yes'. If you need me to witness, my answer is 'yes'. If you need me to preach, my answer is 'yes'. If you need me to stand with someone, my answer is 'yes'. If you tell me to forgive my enemy, my answer is 'yes'. If you tell me to go back to school, my answer is 'yes'. Let your answer be, "Yes!"

I Made It Out

My plans for my life were so different than what God had for me. I was convinced that I was called to be a hometown attorney. But God called me to be a pastor and a preacher. I wanted no parts of ministry. One day I was arrested by the will of God and walked directly into purpose. I did not want to, but I told him yes. The moment I told God yes, everything that I needed to fulfill purpose became attracted to me.

The highest praise you can give God is not with your mouth, but with your surrender. Isaiah 43:21 (KJV) *"This people have I formed for myself; they shall shew forth my praise."* We were fashioned for the express purpose of showing forth praise to our Creator. In our surrender, we are doing exactly what we were created to do. This is the highest form of worship.

When you give the Lord your life, it can be messy. God does not just want to make your gift shine. He wants to make every part of you, whole. Your yes, requires your entire life's journey. In your yes is your fulfillment and the beginning of miracles. It is the key that opens the doors that lead to new spaces and places.

Volume Two

God is going to use your, yes to change the world. The breakthrough that you are about to get will not only be for you but for everyone attached to you. I declare that you are one yes away from the floodgates of favor opening. You do not have to understand it. Just agree with God. This yes is going to change everything and cause swift shifts in your direction.

-Bishop Randy Borders

CHAPTER 15: TRUST HIM

Volume Two

Proverbs 3:5-6 (KJV) *"Trust in the Lord with all thine heart; and lean not unto thine own understanding. In all thy ways acknowledge him, and he shall direct thy paths."*

In this passage, King Solomon, son of King David, conveys our trust, reliance, and dependence solely should be on Jehovah. Our acts must not be half-hearted. As children of the Highest, we must trust Him wholeheartedly. This means we are to trust God with our entire being our hearts, mind, soul, and spirit. The heart denotes the center of physical, emotional, intellectual, and moral activities.

With our bodies we are to trust God. In our spirit, trust him. In our soul, mind, flesh, and emotions we are to trust God fully for all area of our lives. When we trust God, He provides wisdom and understanding. Not only does the Lord provide wisdom and understanding, we must recognize His importance in our lives. The Lord is to be the central focal point in turn He brings direction and guidance to our path.

I am a single mother of two beautiful children. I have a teenage son and a preteen daughter. Not once would I have ever imagined that this would be my journey. I grew up in the church. I knew 'church'. At

Volume Two

the time, I thought I had a real relationship with God. It was not until 2007, that things did an entire 180°!

July of 2007, my faith was tested on a different level. My children's father was brutally murdered. What was I to do? How would I cope? As a 23-year-old young woman, with a two-year-old son and eight months pregnant. How was I to take care of these children? So many questions began to infiltrate my mind. "God, why would you allow this to happen to me? I serve you, I sing, I minster to your people and assist wherever help is needed. Why?" These are just a few of the questions that continuously filled my heart and mind.

Previously, I experienced pain. The pain of losing the man with whom I bore children at a young age, was a different level. Even through the pain, there was a press in my heart. My mind and spirit drew me closer to God. Amid pain, there was so much confusion that began to manifest. I got to a place where I quieted my spirit.

Proverbs 3:5-6, a verse I memorized as a child, became my mantra. It was a daily reminder, my declaration. During this period of my life, I began to learn whom God was and how to trust Him. Being in a position of trusting Him had nothing to do with what I could receive from God. It was to know who He was and is for myself.

In this season of my life, I learned how to give it honestly and wholeheartedly all to the Father. I trusted Him with my life, children, finances, to supply my needs, and so much more. As I learned to trust God, my eyes were opened. He began to supply me with His wisdom and understanding. He supplied and supplies me with so much peace and joy. It causes my steps and His plans to become immersed with one another. It caused me to see things much clearer for my life!

When we as God's children learn how to trust Him wholeheartedly, not to lean to our own understanding. We reap the benefit, which is direction! I found there is no wavering with God. He is steady, consistent, stable, and most of all faithful. He always comes through! Life has a way of throwing many blows. When your trust is rooted in God, you realize an understanding and an awareness. Life's blows are designed to strengthen you in the Lord.

Volume Two

What area or areas in your life have you not totally surrendered to God? I admonish you today and every day, give it over to the Lord. Trust, He will do what He said He would do pertaining to you. Regardless of the issue, storm, test, or trial learn to trust God wholeheartedly. He will direct your path. Despite it all, trust in God. He will not ever let you down!

-Minister Ebony Marie Petty

CHAPTER 16: TAKE THE RISK

Volume Two

Romans 4:19-21 (KJV) *"And being not weak in faith, he considered not his own body now dead, when he was about a hundred years old, neither yet the deadness of Sara's womb: He staggered not at the promise of God through unbelief; but was strong in faith, giving glory to God; And being fully persuaded that, what He had promised, He was able also to perform."*

In television, film, and theatre, typecasting is the process by which an actor strongly identifies with a specific character. There may be one or more specific roles or characters having the same traits. They may be of the same social or ethnic group. When typecasting, one must place be confident in the role they elect to embody; in their ability to engulf themselves in the role.

Ultimately, this requires faith in oneself and willingness to take a risk. Knowing they may wholeheartedly succeed or fail. The very thought of this is a scary notion for some, perhaps even many. Willingness to take risks is not comfortable for mankind. If a hundred people who failed to reach their life goals were polled, at least eighty would reason their lack of success was due to being afraid to take a particular risk.

I humbly say that risk-taking is a specific characteristic in which I strongly believe in and identify. I have been a risk-taker for most of my life. It came second nature to me. I realized; in life you are never going to achieve real success unless you are willing to take risks. Risk is defined as the possibility of suffering harm, loss, or danger.

The reason most people will not take a risk is the fear of losing. Instead, they play it safe. They do grant themselves an opportunity to embrace the possibility of massive success. Anyone who has enjoyed any measure of success will tell you, they had to take some form of a risk. There was a possibility of losing it all. However, that same leap of faith can catapults you far beyond the level of success that you could dream or imagine.

In November of 1991, I was called to full-time ministry at Second Unity Full Gospel Church. Pastor Kim Davis, to whom I was married, said to me, "Don't worry about anything. Financially, I got us. Build the ministry and I will do my part." That leap of faith laid the foundation for our future success. I took a risk and it paid off, not just for me but for everyone that benefited from my ministry.

In September of 1994, Bishop Paul S. Morton, Sr. came to our church to minister at a crusade. At that time, he was the founder of a new organization called the Full Gospel Baptist Church Fellowship. I was offered to be a part of this organization without attending the first conference. Unbeknownst to me, I accepted an invitation to one of the most prominent organizations in Christianity. I simply had taken a risk and it paid off!

My whole life has been a 'faith walk'. I have not punched a '9 to 5' time clock in almost 30 years. I lived by faith and not sight. Faith, the evidence of things not seen is the risk that paid off!

Two primary reasons we do not take risks are fear and doubt. What helps us to move forward is the seed of faith. Without faith, being a risk-taker is simply impossible. Faith requires you to believe in what you do not see. The only solution to choose is to act on a seed of faith. To be a risk-taker, we must follow the formula of the original risk taker, Father Abraham. Do not be weak in faith.

What does it mean to be weak in faith? To understand, we must understand that faith is more than simply believing. It is a principle of action based upon one's belief. Does one sit in a chair and check for its stability beforehand? I have never seen it done! Does one go to work daily without expecting a paycheck? Absolutely, not!

Faith and action must align in the spiritual realm with God as it does in our daily lives. Faith, or lack of faith, begins in the mind. Your actions will align with the thoughts that you can conceive and believe. Faith means to believe in what you cannot physically see with the naked eye. Faith is spiritual power. The only way to activate it is to begin moving or acting upon what you do not see. Being strong in faith is having the spiritual strength to move on what you trust, based on the conception of the thoughts in your mind.

Therefore, being weak in faith is simply the opposite. Non-belief and not acting upon what your mind cannot conceive. Being weak in faith means being afraid to commit to action. You have not placed trust in the Lord and His promises. You have not placed faith in the promise that He has already ordered your steps. This does not mean that you have no faith. It may mean you are not strong yet.

Having weak faith simply means that you do not possess enough spiritual insight to take necessary actions to manifest what you see spiritually into the natural realm. This can delay or hinder what you are anticipating in prayer. It is an indication that your faith walk lacks the necessary experience. The more you act on what you trust, the stronger your faith will become. Strong faith is the foundation of becoming a risk-taker! Do not consider your situation or circumstance.

> Hebrews 11:17-19 (ESV) *"By faith Abraham, when he was tested, offered up Isaac, and he who had received the promises was in the act of offering up his only son, of whom it was said, 'Through Isaac shall your offspring be named.' He considered that God was able even to raise him from the dead, from which, figuratively speaking, he did receive him back."*

After God promised Abraham future generations through Isaac, He made him wait many years for the birth of Isaac. Abraham had taken steps to fulfill this promise with the help of his wife Sarah. Sarah being of weak faith, offered her handmaid, Hagar. As a surrogate mother, Hagar was to conceive a son as man's attempt to fulfill the Lord's promise.

Notice the scripture states, 'by faith.' Faith requires you to 'see' (spiritually) what you cannot 'see' (physically). It also requires you to not be moved by what you 'do' see (physically). Sarah was moved by the natural circumstance around her.

In the walk of faith, your situation or circumstance that is visible to the physical eye cannot be your guiding force. Choose to walk in faith. Abraham, like many patriarchs of faith, trusted God. He did not consider the situation or circumstances. The only outcome he was expecting was God's Word. He was willing to risk it all. We must make the same decision. Do not stagger in what God promised you because of unbelief.

> Abraham went to the mountain designated by God, built the altar, spread the wood, and bound his son. But when he raised the knife, at the last possible second, God intervened and said, *"Do not lay your hand on the boy... do anything to him... Now I know that you fear God."* (Genesis 22:12 NIV).

Talk about a risk-taker! Can any of us say that we are strong in faith to sacrifice in obedience to God? Could we sacrifice something or someone we love dearly? The more steps you take in faith, the stronger you will be. You will believe in His Word and refute all thoughts of unbelief. Believe that God is going to do His part and perform what He said He would.

> Joshua 21:43, 45 (KJV) *"So the Lord gave to Israel all the land of which He had sworn to give to their fathers, and they took possession of it and dwelt in it. Not a word failed of any good thing which the Lord had spoken to the house of Israel. All came to pass."*

> Deuteronomy 19:8-9 (KJV) *"Now if the Lord your God enlarges your territory, as He swore to your fathers, and gives you the land which He promised to give to your fathers... Then you shall add three more cities for yourself besides these three."*

God's Word cannot fail. We must make the decision that He can be trusted. Taking risks is not for the faint at heart. There is a possibility that it may not work the way we think it should. We may not succeed the first time. There is also a strong possibility that it may work perfectly. The question is, are you willing to take a risk? It may shift the course of your entire life for the better. You could very well be a step away from a defining moment of your career, ministry, or life. I encourage you to step out and begin what you have been called to do. Take the risk!

-Bishop Greg Davis

Volume Two

CHAPTER 17: I FORGIVE YOU

Volume Two

"If we don't disciple people, the culture sure will," a quote from Dr. Leonard Sweet, modern day theologian.

Humanity is always on a quest to know and discover. Our very lives byproducts of how we navigate the crossroads between question and curiosity to forge awareness. On this journey, we acquire knowledge. Hopefully, it leads to growth, maturity, and ideals necessary to embrace who the Father created us to be. We must submit to a Godly mindset as His people. Lest we be taught by men still grasping at truth; arrogantly asserting their opinionated discoveries as truth.

It is my strong belief that bad definitions lead to wrong destinations. To misunderstand a concept is also to misapply a principle. Ignorance is not bliss. What you do not know may be what you need to bless you. We must seek to understand what may yet be difficult to comprehend and live. A difficult principle to grasp is forgiveness. As difficult as it is to comprehend, it is also one of the most essential to understand. It plainly dictates how God will interact with us in relationship.

> *"For if you forgive other people when they sin against you, your heavenly Father will also forgive you. But if you do not forgive*

others their sins, your Father will not forgive your sins." Matthew 6:14-15 NIV

What is really at the core of forgiveness? What is the standard? Can it truly ever be merited? What is the Father's objective for us with forgiveness? What does it reveal? As we embark upon this curious journey together, let us remain open. Allow the Father to speak to you; knowing that everything He reveals is His truest essence, love. *"Greater love has no one than this: to lay down one's life for one's friends."* John 15:13 (NIV).

Love is such a great responsibility. It is truly the most sacrificial decision one can make. There is no love without placing yourself in a position, an expectation with the possibility of being disappointed. Love is not for the weak. Not for the wayward or taciturn. It is committed through tears. It forgives in pain. It tries again until it is rejected. Even then, it hopes. It is not stupid or clueless. To the contrary, it knows. It sees the faults but believes the future.

Many of the things we say we cannot get over lies in expectation. We expect of others a standard that does not accommodate their faults. Love is a more excellent way that does not seek perfection. It looks for the opportunity to recover God's image and likeness in every situation. Moving in love gives us insight. We learn why God 'fore-gives' Jesus so He can forgive us. He is prepared for fault and frailty. Forgiveness is love in motion to maintain freedom. The liberty to move forward in a progressive relationship after hurt or failure occurred.

To be free to function in God's will, our hearts must maintain a level of purity. Regardless of the pain and hurt that we experience, purity makes it feasible to hear and sense the divine intimations (pulse) of His voice. One of the diminishing enemies of purity is hatred. Hatred taints the lens of the heart. It renders it blind, incapable of recognizing the value and worth of another.

Hatred makes us forgetful of our own shortcomings to render others unforgivable for theirs. It spews venom on the success of others. Yet, it covets the possessions of others. Avoid it at all cost. We must wrap ourselves in God's love. Allow Him to place that love in our heart. Let His love be our official 'language'. Speak it to each other daily.

Volume Two

    Love is the 'cornerstone' of forgiveness. It is the choice to "lay down our lives" so others can continue to live. Forgiveness is a 'death'. It brings life out of a confusing pain. It causes us to resemble God. It is necessary for restoration to take place. It is, as the songwriter, Andrae Crouch wrote, "[To] look beyond faults and see the need."

> *"Father, forgive them for they know not what they do."* (Luke 23:34). But what do you do when they know what they are doing? Do they ever really know?

    It is difficult to access a greater conscience and remain conscious. To forgive, we in a sense lose our minds. Do we detach from the pain, absolving the guilty of their sin and its penalty? Or do we allow the Spirit to transport our heart and mind to a transcending place? Do we utilize the pain as a bridge? It is inevitable to be confronted with the idea of forgiving someone who will never experience the chaos they afflicted upon you.

    History proves that at any given moment, life will purposely afflict you through a cycle. What happens when the forgiven make transgression the law of the land? With the backdrop of entitled arrogance, they expect you to forgive them; to wipe the slate clean.

Only they do not stop, they continue to scribble on the slate with more mistreatment.

It may seem tiresome. To feel we spoiled the transgressor. Perhaps, we feel we outsmarted them. We proved how blind and weak they are in their inability to see our value or worth in their lives. There can be an endless trail of necessary relationships, broken and destroyed because of forgiveness' inability to change people's behavior.

Can forgiveness be given prematurely? Are we to assure ourselves that the transgressor acknowledges their act? Shall they repent of their ways before we say, "You are forgiven?" Did Joseph forgive his brothers while experiencing the purposefully wicked pain they caused him? Or did he let them starve to death in the famine? Did he allow them to reap the fruit of their actions before his heart made room to release and love them?

Those who are called to be saviors and deliverers are often bear the burden of forgiving. They must render the most diabolical as deficient. The most intentionally hurtful, as ignorantly halted in their own mind. My friend, this is indeed a hard row to hoe. Make no mistake, those with the ability to forgive are intimidating to some. Not because of any presupposed brute physical strength. It is not even the eternal portion of our endowed creativity.

It is the ability to transcend the 'trash' intended to hurt us. It is the ability to tap into the Divine. Find strength to sing a joyous song in sorrow. Dance in a dungeon. Pray for our enemy. When you love a loser, believe Heaven hears our hearts in hell. See progress and promise while locked in prison.

It is the 'edge' forgiveness yields. It is the capacity not to allow hatred to reduce us to the lowest common denominator of humanity's underbelly. The truth is there are people who will know exactly how they are hurting you. Their actions were cold, calculated, and consistent. Forgiveness gives us the ability to use the lowdown as an elevator to a higher place in life, liberty, love, and God.

Allow forgiveness to impart wisdom. Do not go bankrupt trying to 'pay' someone back who hurt you. Life has a treasury that is never depleted. Be assured. They will reap. If not on this side of time, on the other.

> *"Do not be deceived: God cannot be mocked." A man reaps what he sows. Whoever sows to please their flesh, from the flesh will reap destruction; whoever sows to please the Spirit, from the Spirit will reap eternal life."* (Galatians 6:7-8).

Forgiveness is not just for person who committed the wrong. It is an 'escape hatch' for those who have been hurt. Allowing them to get out of the way, the principle of reciprocity fulfills itself. 'Forgive and forget' is one of the most enduring clichés of all times. It is what we tell those confronted with the holding onto toxic grudges and dispositions. They have the potential to eat away the very fabric of our being.

Forgiveness is prescribed to the injured. It does not allow their pain of the moment to endure. Hurt limits the forward movement of our lives. It lays the onus of a painful happening on the victim. They then carry the total burden of the situation. Many who offer advice rarely tell the hurt how to forget. What is the process of not remembering the pain? Is this even possible? Maybe it is. Does God require it? Perhaps, remembering is the only way we can keep forgiving.

Volume Two

To 'forgive and forget' does not mean to remove totally from the mind. It means to remove from the motive of the next decision. It is power not to allow what happened in our past affect our next decisions. It is the ability to express love towards the one whom may have hurt us. To forget is to reprogram the mind. It is processing the moment through the Holy Spirit. Inevitably, see the transgression as God sees it; profitable for learning, living, and loving.

We never truly forget. We, like God, simply choose not to remember. We do not put the puzzled pieces of the painful event back together again and relive it. We embrace the opportunity to share your heart. If we live in fear of repeated trauma, it causes us to reject God's grace. We choose to move beyond an incident, to live a life free from heart contamination.

Fear has torment. It places us in a cyclical 'hell'. It imprisons our ability to love fully; always looking over our shoulders for sabotage. Forgetting never truly wipes our mental slate clean. It does, however, cause us to remember the times God erased our own personal mess from His mind. Mercy triumphed over judgment. Forgetting is remembering God has chosen to forget our transgressions. We can have the same mercy on others. The mercy that daily meets us every morning. Do not forget to remember, the Lord forgives.

> *"Because of the Lord's great love we are not consumed, for his compassions never fail. They are new every morning; great is your faithfulness. The Lord is my portion; therefore I will wait for him."* (Lamentations 3:21-24)

- Minister L. Spenser Smith

Volume Two

About the Author

All the teachers and preachers represented in this opus have either spoken into my life or I enjoy their ministry. They speak from the heart and represent the title of this work, "I Made It Out". The varying ages and denominations of the contributing authors targets a wide range demographic. My aim is not to cater to a certain demographic. This music and project speak to all generations.

First, I composed the music. After selecting the sequential order of the songs, it hit me like a ton of bricks! The order seemed to have a strong message. I was inspired to create chapters from these titles. I believed they would encourage and speak to the heart of all the people who embraced my music. Because of my success in the music industry, I pray and believe the impact of the book will be comparable. This book shares insight and solutions for the issues the church struggles with daily. I am looking forward to witnessing a harvest from this work.

The desire to release this book came immediately after the musical project was completed. It was my goal to have this book available for our 2020 tour. I want to provide my audience of fans to receive the whole "I Made It Out" experience. I pray that I inspire the masses. So many supported my literary projects in the past. It is my prayer that this body of work will cause my followers to reach, read, reflect, and be blessed!

"I Made It Out," is a declaration. In some ways, it is the sequel to the hit song, "Life and Favor, You Don't Know My Story". Everybody has a story. Some have absolutely no desire to tell it. Still I knew that would not shut down the spirit of their testimony. "I Made It Out", speaks to all survived of our respective past. It speaks to the things surrendered to God.

When you listen to or read, "I Made It Out", it becomes a personal declaration that you can scream from the mountain tops or enjoy in the seat of your car. Either way, something about that declaration represents joy! It allows you to know; if God did it before, that same God will do it again!

Made in the USA
Monee, IL
07 November 2021